Move like a
LION

By Radzi Chinyanganya

Illustrations by Francesca Rosa

Sport has always been a HUGE part of my life; from memories of watching the Olympics on TV with my Dad, to sliding headfirst down an ice-track in my quest to become a Team GB Winter Olympian in Skeleton-Bobsleigh (I failed), or even eventually anchoring that same Winter Olympics Games which I'd once dreamt of competing in for the BBC.

Growing up, I went to six different schools and lived in six different houses, so I was used to being the "new kid". But sport has always given me confidence, because I knew that on my first day at a new school, I would only have to wait until breaktime to feel welcome. As it was then that people would see that I was good at the activity we played, and next time they would want me on their team.

However, as much as I love sport, I know it can also exclude, discourage, and demoralise. So I made this book, to do the exact opposite; to improve how you feel, to challenge you, to encourage you, to inspire you, and to do so with movement.

Before you start reading and start moving, thank you for choosing my book, and for allowing me to share my passion with you.

BEFORE YOU START

Have fun doing the exercises but please remember not to overdo it, particularly where you find some of the moves difficult – everyone is good at different things. Just do what you are comfortable with, and what feels right for you. Ask an adult to help you with some of the trickier moves.

ADVICE TO PARENTS

Any physical exercise has risk of injury, and every child is different. Please be aware of your child's personal limitations, and provide any necessary help.

CONTENTS

DIFFICULTY

Each of the movements has been graded based on difficulty. Simply look for this star rating on each page.

EASY   MEDIUM   HARD

DISCLAIMER The exercises in this book have been comprehensively researched and we have made all reasonable efforts to ensure that they are safe for children to undertake. However, any physical exercise carries a risk of injury, and parents are advised to ensure that any exercise their child undertakes is within any physical limitations they may have. The publisher will not accept any liability for any injury or damage arising to anyone who follows the suggestions in this book.

Wake up routine...

Kneel down, then lean over with your arms straight in front of you and touch the floor. Rest your forehead on the floor.

Sit up with your legs crossed. Rest your hands on your knees.

Move your right hand to your left knee and use it to gently twist your body to the left. Repeat on the other side.

Perform this short routine after waking up to get physically and mentally ready for the day ahead. Hold each pose for about 20 seconds.

Concentrate on deep breathing throughout.
Inhaling and exhaling slowly through your nose.

Sit with one foot pulled toward your groin and the other leg extended. Rest your forehead on your leg and try to touch your foot.

Repeat with your other leg.

Cross your legs and extend your arms forward, touching the floor in front of you.

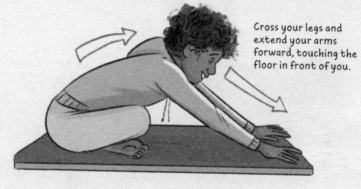

Lay flat on your back and pull your feet in toward your groin. Extend your arms straight out to the side.

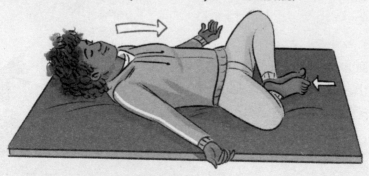

Move your feet shoulder-width apart. Press the bottom of your feet onto the floor and lift your hips.

Cross your left leg over your right leg. Interlock your fingers around your right knee and pull it toward your chest. Repeat on the other side.

Swing your legs...

With your arms at your side, swing your legs up to the sky.

Pull your right knee over your left leg while keeping your other leg straight. Repeat on the other side.

Did you know?
You can perform this routine any time, but it's a great way to start the day!

Lay on your back and place your arms at your sides. Close your eyes and relax for a few minutes and focus on your breath.

STALK

like a crocodile

These ancient creatures have existed for 95 million years, and were around during the time of the dinosaurs. They are master hunters in the water, but are **surprisingly fast** when they run on land, too.

Did you know?
Crocodiles have the strongest bite of any animal in the world.

Grrr...

Crocodile walk

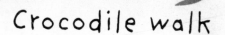

Begin in a press-up position with your arms slightly turned out.

Dragging your feet behind you, begin to walk forward with your hands using a pulling motion. Your body will sway a bit, which is normal.

Alternating between your right and left hand move yourself forward, using your hands to support your weight. Drag your feet the entire time.

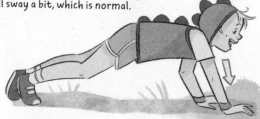

Challenge yourself
Try to keep your body very straight.

SCUTTLE

like a crab

Crabs have ten legs but only walk on eight. The front two pincers are just for gripping. Crabs mostly **walk sideways** because their legs are on the side of their bodies, but they can walk forward slowly too.

Challenge yourself
Try walking slowly or even backwards.

Crab walk

Start by sitting on the floor with your arms behind your back and your bottom off the ground.

Keep your knees hip-distance apart.

Lift your hips up so your body makes the shape of a table.

Walk forward by moving your left arm, then right leg, followed by your right arm and left leg. Try to keep your bottom up and your body flat.

WIGGLE

like a worm

Because earthworms don't have limbs, they burrow through the soil by **changing shape**. They stretch the front of their bodies then grip the earth with tiny invisible bristles while the rear part follows.

Slow worm

STRENGTHENS YOUR ARMS, SHOULDERS, AND LEGS.

Start in a bent over position with your feet close together and your fingertips touching the floor, shoulder-width apart.

Slowly walk your hands forward.

12

When you feel comfortable, stop moving your hands and place your palms on the floor.

Slowly walk your feet forward to meet your hands. When you feel comfortable, stop moving your feet.

Did you know?

Worms have no eyes, ears, or nose, but can sense light and vibrations.

Repeat the process by walking your hands forward again.

Challenge yourself

Try holding the flat position for as long as you can.

13

Worm dance

STRENGTHENS YOUR ARMS
AND CORE MUSCLES.

Begin by kneeling in an upright position with
your hips over your knees. Then fall forward into
a press up, catching yourself with your hands.

As you catch yourself,
bend your knees.

Kick your feet down
towards the floor.

As this creates momentum through your back, push the floor with your hands.

Fall forward again and repeat the process.

Try doing a number of "worms" in a row.

Challenge yourself
Try to make the moves as smooth as possible.

15

BALANCE

like a flamingo

Flamingos are masters at balancing, and **sleep on one leg for hours at a time**. The reason for this is that being on one leg with their head and necks flopped on their back takes less effort for their muscles than standing on two legs.

Did you know?

The reason flamingos are pink is because they eat pink shrimp and algae.

Flamingo extension

STRENGTHENS YOUR LEGS
AND CORE CORE MUSCLES.

Stand on one leg with
the other slightly bent
to help you balance.

Slowly extend your
bent leg backwards.

Focus on something in front
of you to help you balance.

Challenge yourself
Try jumping on your
supporting leg.

Repeat with
the other leg.

CRAWL

like a caterpillar

Caterpillars are the young of butterflies and moths. Before they are ready to turn into butterflies and flutter about, they mostly just crawl around on leaves **eating as much as they can**!

Slow caterpillar

STRENGTHENS YOUR ARMS, LEGS, AND CORE MUSCLES.

Start bent over with your feet together and your hands on the floor.

Did you know?

Caterpillars are eating machines, and spend almost all their time munching leaves.

Slowly walk your feet backward, keeping your hands still.

When you feel comfortable, stop moving your feet and place the balls of your feet on the floor.

Slowly walk your hands back to meet your feet.

Challenge yourself
Try holding the flat position for as long as you can.

Begin walking your feet again to repeat.

19

FLAP

like a butterfly

Butterflies begin life as caterpillars. Once a caterpillar eats enough food, it transforms into a **pupa** and forms a **case** around itself. After a while it emerges as a butterfly that flaps and flutters between flowers in search of **nectar**.

Flutter

Flutter

Did you know?

Butterflies can't fly if they drop below a certain temperature.

Flutter

Butterfly flaps

STRENGTHENS
YOUR CORE MUSCLES.

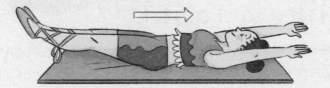

Start by laying flat on your back with your arms above your head.

While keeping your bottom on the floor, lift your head, arms, and feet.

This will create a "V" shape.

Split your hands and feet apart to make a star shape – almost as if you are opening and closing a set of wings.

Challenge yourself
Try making the V shape narrower.

HOP

like a rabbit

These cute creatures have some clever ways to avoid predators. Not only are they fast, but their ears can detect even the **slightest of sounds**, and they can see in almost all directions at once.

Bunny hops

STRENGTHENS YOUR
LEGS, ARMS, AND BACK.

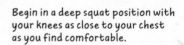

Begin in a deep squat position with your knees as close to your chest as you find comfortable.

Hold your arms out in front of you, keeping your chest up.

Lean forward until your hands touch the floor in front of you.

Let your arms support your body weight and hop up with your feet.

Challenge yourself

Try increasing the size of the hop.

HOP

HOP

23

WADDLE

like a duck

Ducks are strong **swimmers**, **skilled divers**, **and graceful fliers**, but on ground they can look a little… funny. However, if you copy their walk it's a great way to exercise your legs and improve your balance!

Duck walk

STRENGTHENS YOUR CORE MUSCLES AND LEGS.

Quack! Quack!

Begin walking in a straight line, taking short, slow steps.

With every stride you take, gradually duck down a little.

Did you know?
Ducks produce a special oil to make their feathers waterproof.

Keeping your body upright, duck lower and lower with each step, bringing your bottom closer to your feet.

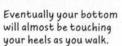

Eventually your bottom will almost be touching your heels as you walk.

By this stage, only the balls of your feet should be making contact with the ground.

Bend your arms and point your elbows out to the side to show off your wings!

Challenge yourself
Try walking slowly or even backwards.

BEND

like an octopus

Octopuses are one of the strangest and most amazing animals on Earth. They have eight limbs, three hearts, nine brains, blue blood, and no bones. Having no bones makes them **bendy enough** to squeeze into tiny spots.

Octopus bridge

Begin laying face up on the the floor with your knees bent.

STRENGTHENS YOUR BACK, ARMS, AND SHOULDERS.

Bend your arms so your elbows point up, and place your palms flat on the floor by your head.

Ask an adult to support your weight. Then, keeping your hands and feet in the same position, push down into the floor, lifting your hips up.

Did you know?
Each of an octopus's limbs has its own mini brain!

See how high you can raise your hips.

Challenge yourself
Try bringing your feet and hands as close together as you can.

Hold the position, then carefully lower back down.

STING

★★ MEDIUM

like a scorpion

Scorpions are best known for their terrifying tails. When they locate their prey they grab it in their pincers and unleash a lightning-fast strike with their tail that **delivers a deadly venomous sting**.

Tail whips

STRENGTHENS YOUR LEGS, ARMS, SHOULDERS, AND CORE MUSCLES

Begin in a relaxed press-up position with your arms and legs shoulder-width apart.

Sightly twist your hips to the right, then bend your right knee, bringing it in toward your hands.

Keeping your right leg bent, swing it out to the right and around the back of your supporting left leg.

Challenge yourself
Try making the width between your hands and feet narrower.

Hold this position, then return to the original press-up position. Repeat with your other leg.

Tail whip transitions

★★★
HARD

STRENGTHENS YOUR ARMS, SHOULDERS, AND BACK.

Begin with your hands and feet on the floor, your body facing up, and your bottom off the floor.

Swing one arm over your body so it will land on the other side from the other, about shoulder-width apart.

While your arm is swinging, begin the same movement with the same leg so it whips around.

Land your foot about shoulder-width apart on the other side of your other foot.

Your body should now be facing down. Repeat this process to get back to your starting position, then keep going!

Challenge yourself

Try making the movements as quickly as you can.

HIDE

like a tortoise

Tortoises are perhaps best-known for their shells. These tough domes on their backs grant tortoises an impressive defensive skill. If they feel threatened, they can **pull their head and necks inside** their shells for protection.

Tortoise hide

STRENGTHENS YOUR LEGS AND CORE MUSCLES.

Lay face down on a mat or blanket with your arms and legs spread as wide as you can.

Bend your arms and knees, bringing your hands and feet in towards your body.

HANG
like a bat

Did you know?
Bats are the only mammals capable of true flight.

Bats are famous for hanging upside down. They do this because they can't take off from the ground. Instead, they climb to high places, hang, and **fall into flight**. The ability to hang also lets them rest in safe places such as tall branches, or the ceilings of caves.

Bat headstand

Begin by kneeling on a mat or soft surface with plenty of space around you.

Slowly lean forward and place your arms, elbows, and head on the floor in front of you.

Walk your feet away from your head until your legs have a slight bend in them.

Carefully raise your legs above your head. Try this against a wall to practice it first.

Challenge yourself
Try lowering your legs to the floor and lifting them back up.

35

BEND
like a dolphin

Most of the time, bottlenose dolphins swim quite slowly, but if they quickly **bend their bodies and tails**, they create enough force to cover short distances in very quick bursts.

Did you know?

Dolphins are very intelligent. Experts believe they can even recognize themselves in a mirror.

Dolphin dorsal lift

STRENGTHENS YOUR
LEGS, BACK, AND SHOULDERS.

Start laying face down on the
floor with your your arms
extended in front of you.

Keeping your legs and arms straight,
lift them off the ground and hold that
position for as long as you can.

Lower your arms and legs back to the
floor, take a short rest, then repeat.

Challenge yourself
Try lifting your
hands and feet
as high as you can.

PLAY

like a dog

Dogs are **playful**, **intelligent**, **and loyal**, which is why they make such beloved pets. There are more than 400 different breeds of dog – that's a lot of furry friends!

Roll over

STRENGTHENS YOUR CORE MUSCLES.

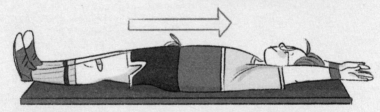

Start laying face-up on the floor with your arms extended above you.

Keeping your legs and arms completely straight,
rotate your body so you face downwards.

Did you know?

A dog's sense of smell can be more than 10,000 times more sensitive than a human's.

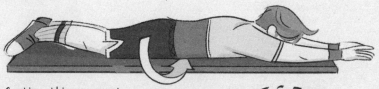

Continue this movement
so you go back to facing up.

Repeat this, and try going
in both directions.

Challenge yourself

Try not to let your legs or arms touch the floor.

Lazy dog

STRENGTHENS YOUR CORE MUSCLES.

Start in press-up position with your arms shoulder-width apart and your knees on the floor.

Slightly turn your hands out.

Begin to walk with your hands. Start with one hand and place it comfortably in front of its original position.

Put most of your bodyweight on that hand and push yourself forward with it, whilst lifting your other hand up and placing that forward.

Switch hands and repeat the process, dragging your legs behind you.

Challenge yourself
Try to keep your body in a straight line, from your shoulders to your knees.

SPRINT
like an ostrich

★★
MEDIUM

The ostrich is the world's largest bird. They can't fly, but they can run **very fast**. In fact, thanks to their **extremely powerful legs** they're the fastest two-legged animal in the world.

Let's go!

Did you know?
Although ostriches can't fly, their wings aren't useless – they use them for balance while running!

straight leg sprints

STRENGTHENS YOUR
LEGS AND CORE MUSCLES.

Start by standing upright and
jogging on the spot. Try to get
your knees nice and high!

Do this until you feel nice and
loose and have a good rhythm.

Start swinging your legs in
front of you, keeping them
straight the whole time.

Use the motion of
your arms to help
swing your legs higher.

Challenge yourself
Try keeping your
hands by your sides.

Finally, gradually allow your
contact with the ground
to propel you forward.

STAND

like a meerkat

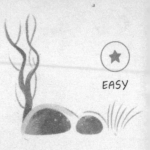
Meerkats live underground and only come out of their burrows in the morning. They walk on all fours, but are famous for **standing up** on their hind legs so they can spot predators in the distance.

What's over there?

Did you know?

Meerkats take turns guarding their home. If one of them sees a predator they alert the rest of the group.

Meerkat squats

Start standing upright with your feet shoulder-width apart and your arms out in front of you.

While keeping your chest up, bend your knees until your hips are level with your knees.

Hold that position for a moment, then stand back up.

Challenge yourself

Try varying the width of your feet.

45

SIDEWIND
like a snake

We usually think of snakes slowly slithering on the ground, but some snakes that live in sandy places can move very quickly by using a technique called **sidewinding**.

Did you know?

While sidewinding, snakes can move at up to 30kph!

Sandsnake sidewind

Start by standing with your arms at your side. Place your left leg slightly in front of your right.

Swing your arms and hips back, bending your right knee, straightening your left, and slightly tipping your chest forward. Then in a continuous motion...

Swing your arms and hips backward.

Straighten both legs and arch your back from the waist.

Swing your hips again and keep repeating like a dance.

47

WRIGGLE

like a centipede

Although the word centipede means "100 legs", most centipedes have about 35 pairs, and some have as few as 15. You might not think it to look at them, but centipedes can run **very fast**.

Did you know?

Centipedes can regrow lost legs!

Centipede V-sits

Start on your back with your
arms above your head.

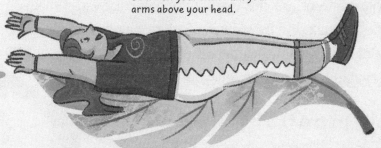

While keeping your
bottom on the floor,
lift your head, arms, and
legs to make a V-shape.

Touch the highest part
of your legs you can
comfortably reach.

Lower back down to
the floor and repeat.

Challenge yourself
Try making the
V-shape narrower,
and reach up higher.

SNEAK

like a chimpanzee

Chimpanzees are our closest animals relatives. They get around by climbing and swinging through trees and by **walking on all fours**, but are also able to walk upright like humans.

Chimpanzee sneak

STRENGTHENS YOUR CORE MUSCLES.

Did you know?

Chimpanzees are one of the only animals known to use tools.

Start by kneeling in an upright position with the balls of your feet on the floor, and your bottom on your feet.

Lift your right knee and place your foot flat on the floor near your left knee.

Push your right knee to the floor, bringing the right foot onto its ball.

At the same time, allow your left foot to naturally fall inward, and your left knee to move away from the hip.

Challenge yourself
Try moving as quickly as you can.

Leading with the knee, lift your left leg off the floor, swing it around to the front, and place your left foot in front of your right.

51

ROLL
like a hedgehog

Hedgehogs are famous for their **prickly spines**. These spines help protect hedgehogs from predators, and are found over their entire bodies except for their face, legs, and underbelly.

Did you know?
When hedgehogs are born their spines are soft. They only harden as they get older.

I'm sleeping...

Hedgehog ball

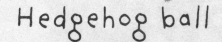

STRENGTHENS YOUR
CORE MUSCLES.

Sit on the floor with your
knees bent, then bring
your feet as close to your
bottom as you can.

Tightly wrap your arms
around your knees and tuck
your head into your chest.

Staying in this shape, allow
yourself to naturally roll
onto your back and sides.

Challenge yourself
Try rolling yourself
into a tighter ball.

53

STALK
like a lion

To hunt successfully, **lions must go unnoticed**.
If they are seen or heard their prey will run away.
Lions use the long grass to their advantage by blending
in and waiting for the perfect time to strike.

Did you know?

Lions are fast but get tired quickly. They save energy by moving slowly and staying low to the ground.

54

Lion creep

STRENGTHENS YOUR ARMS, LEGS, AND BACK.

Start crouched on all fours. Keep your legs bent with your knees and the balls of both feet on the floor.

While keeping low, push forward with your left foot, moving your right leg forward.

Shhh! Quietly...

Slide your left hand forward.

Crouch deeper, getting closer to the floor, then repeat on the other side, staying as low and quiet as you can.

Challenge yourself
Try pausing for extended periods.

PROWL

like a cat

Cats are popular house pets who love to snooze, but they have great balance and agility that helps them hunt. When cats walk they **follow a sequence**. They move their back foot, followed by the front foot on the same side.

Did you know?

Giraffes and camels are some of the only other animals to walk in this way.

Cat walk

STRENGTHENS YOUR SHOULDERS AND LEGS.

Start crouched on all fours with your hands shoulder-width apart and your legs slightly bent.

Stand on the balls of your feet.

56

While staying low, push forward with your right foot and slide your right hand forward just above the ground.

Do exactly the same with your left side. Move your left foot, then your left hand.

Repeat this process, staying smooth and slow.

Challenge yourself
Try walking in a straight line as if you are on a tightrope.

HOP

like a kangaroo

kangaroos are the only large animal that hop to get around. Kangaroos can cover long distances by using their **powerful legs and tail**, but don't worry – you can do it without a tail!

kangaroo broad jump

STRENGTHENS YOUR LEGS.

Stand with your feet shoulder-width apart, then bend your knees and swing your arms back.

LEAP

like a frog

Frogs have **long**, **powerful** back legs that allow them to leap great distances. Some frogs can jump up to 20 times their own body length in a single leap!

Frog jump

STRENGTHENS YOUR LEGS, ARMS, SHOULDERS, AND BACK.

Begin in a deep squat position with your knees as close to your chest as you find comfortable and your chest up.

Reach forward and place your arms slightly out in front of you.

Take a small jump forward so your feet sit just outside your hands.

With your arms taking your weight and your knees bent, kick your legs up so your feet are in the air, close to your bottom.

Let your feet return to the floor. You should almost be back in your original position.

Challenge yourself
Try extending the size of your jump.

SQUEEZE

like a jellyfish

Jellyfish are mostly made of water, and don't have eyes, brains, bones, or a heart. To move, they drift with the current or **open their bodies** to let water in, then **squeeze** it out, which pushes them forward.

Did you know?

Jellyfish have been drifting through the oceans since before even the dinosaurs existed.

Jellyfish shoulder stand

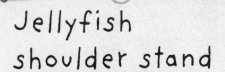

STRENGTHENS YOUR CORE MUSCLES AND LEGS.

Begin by laying on your back with your arms at your side and your feet together.

Swing your legs up and over your head, bending your back and lifting your hips off the floor, creating an "L" shape.

Challenge yourself

If you feel stable enough, try splitting your legs to the sides.

Place your elbows on the floor and support the small of your back with your hands.

Straighten your legs and hold this position for as long as you can.

ROLL

like a panda

Pandas are solitary animals. The only time pandas live together is when a mother is raising her cub. Pandas have almost no natural predators, so spend **almost all their time** sitting around eating bamboo.

Did you know?

Baby pandas are born pink. They grow black and white fur after about three weeks.

Panda rolls

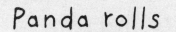

Sit on the floor with your legs apart and straight.

Lean forward and grip the backs of your knees.

Roll towards your left shoulder and twist your hips so your legs swing to the left.

You should end up sitting facing left.

Challenge yourself

Try rolling in the other direction.

Do this three more times to return to your starting position.

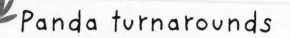

Panda turnarounds

STRENGTHENS YOUR ARMS, SHOULDERS, AND BACK.

Begin with your body facing up, and your hands, feet, and bottom raised off the floor.

Did you know?

Pandas have a special wrist bone they use like a thumb to grip bamboo.

Swing your left arm over your body so it lands on the other side of your right hand about shoulder-width apart.

You can do it!

At the same time, turn your right leg so your entire body faces down.

66

Bring your left leg through and underneath your right leg.

Challenge yourself
Try going as quickly as you can.

This should take you back to your original position.

I'm getting dizzy!

Repeat the process to carry on turning around.

RISE

like a lemur

Lemurs are only found on the tropical island of Madagascar, off the coast of Africa. They are highly skilled climbers, and easily **leap from tree to tree**, using their long arms and tails for balance.

Lemur burpee

STRENGTHENS YOUR CORE MUSCLES, LEGS, AND ARMS.

Start standing with your arms at your side and your feet shoulder-width apart.

Bend down into a deep squat and place the palms of your hands on the floor in front of you.

Did you know?
Baby lemurs can climb trees when they are just three weeks old.

Kick both feet out into press-up position and pause for a second.

And... jump!

Shoot your feet back to the deep squat position, then jump up as high as you can.

Land back in the squat position, then repeat.

Challenge yourself
See how high you can jump at the end.

CRAWL

like a chameleon

These colourful reptiles use their tails like **a fifth limb**. Not only can chameleons use their tails to grip branches, but if they extend them out backwards they help support their bodyweight.

Chameleon walk

STRENGTHENS YOUR CORE MUSCLES, ARMS, AND BACK.

Begin in press-up position with your left arm slightly in front of your right.

Take a step forward with your right foot, so it is level with your hips.

Perform a press-up in that position.

Lift your right hand and your left foot off the floor.

Did you know?
Chameleons can change the colour of their skin.

Perform a two limb press-up, with your arm and leg in the air.

This is tough...

Take a big step forward with your right hand and left foot.

Repeat the process a few times.

Challenge yourself
This one is hard enough alredy!

TWIST

like an orangutan

MEDIUM

Orangutans are the largest animals that live in trees. They have **very long arms** that help them reach branches and swing, but they also use their arms to walk when they venture down to the ground.

Orangutan turnarounds

STRENGTHENS YOUR SHOULDERS AND LEGS.

Begin in a crouched position with your feet together.

Twist your body and place your hands on the floor so they're slightly off to the side.

Keeping your feet together and using your hands to support your weight, jump so your feet land behind your hands.

When you land, your body should be in a straight line.

Twist your body in the other direction and repeat. Try to keep your hands in the same spot.

SHIFT

like a gorilla

These forest dwellers are close relatives of humans. They walk around **on all fours**, and only stand on two legs to fight or to beat their chests as a show of strength and dominance.

Sideways shift

STRENGTHENS YOUR CORE MUSCLES AND SHOULDERS.

Begin in a crouched position with your feet and hands shoulder-width apart.

Shift your hands to the right so your left hand is roughly where your right hand originally was.

74

Did you know?
Young gorillas sleep in trees, but adults are too heavy, so sleep on the ground.

Walk your hands forward at the same time that you jump with your feet. Try to land your feet directly behind your hands.

Repeat this process so your legs shift from side to side as you move forwards.

Challenge yourself
Try moving your hands sideways instead of forwards.

PROWL

like a polar bear

Male polar bears are the **largest land carnivores** in the world, and can weigh as much as ten people! Although they're huge, they're also incredibly fast, and can cover huge amounts of ground in search of food.

Did you know?

Polar bears have an amazing sense of smell, and can sniff out prey under the ice.

Bear walk

STRENGTHENS YOUR LEGS,
SHOULDERS, AND CORE MUSCLES.

Bears move one side of
their body then the other,
so choose a side.

Get into a bent over position, with
your hands and feet on the floor.

Keeping your hips high
and your legs as straight
as possible, lift the foot
of your chosen side off
the ground. As soon as
it's in the air, lift the
arm on the same side.

Move that leg forward to a comfortable
position, followed by your arm. Put down
your foot, then your hand.

Challenge yourself

Try keeping your
legs straight and
your head up.

Keeping your body flat, repeat this action,
switching from one side of the body to the other.

CRAWL
like a spider

MEDIUM

Spiders have eight legs, and can walk in any direction, on walls, and while upside down. Many spiders **spin webs** to trap their prey, but others hunt by sneaking up on prey and **jumping** on them.

Spider crawl

STRENGTHENS YOUR CORE MUSCLES, BACK, AND ARMS.

Start in a press-up position, with your hands shoulder-width apart and your feet slightly wider than that.

Cross your hands and bring your right over your left. Then bring your right foot to meet your left.

Did you know?
Spider legs have fine bristles that detect vibrations, sound, and even smells.

Move your left hand so your arms go back to being shoulder-width apart, then move your left foot back out so you're in your starting position again.

Repeat this process and see how many steps you can take in a row without stopping.

Challenge yourself
Try to keep your body as straight as you can.

79

Jumping spider

STRENGTHENS YOUR CORE
MUSCLES, BACK, AND ARMS.

HARD

Start in a press-up position, with
your hands shoulder-width apart
and your feet slightly wider.

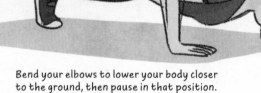

Bend your elbows to lower your body closer
to the ground, then pause in that position.

Did you know?

Jumping spiders
can jump up to 40
times their own
body length!

Lets your hips sink down, and then lift them back up. Practice this a few times until you're comfortable with the movement. Next comes the tricky part.

And...up!

Using the momentum from your hips, push your hands and feet hard into the ground with enough force that your body lifts up, allowing you to raise off the ground.

Challenge yourself
Try doing a number of jumps in a row.

JUMP!

SWING

like an elephant

The African elephant is the **world's largest land animal**. They can grow to be 4 m (13 ft) tall and weigh as much as three cars! These big bodies need a lot of energy, so elephants eat huge amounts of food.

Did you know?

Elephants use their trunks to breathe, gather food, and spray water.

Elephant walk

STRENGTHENS YOUR
CORE MUSCLES.

Start by bending over and letting
your arms hang down in front of you.

Start stepping forward with one
foot as you swing your arms the
other way as if they were a trunk.

Step forward with your
other foot and swing your
arms the other way.

Challenge yourself

Try to keep your legs
as straight as possible
while you walk.

JUMP

like a flea

(★★★) **HARD**

Although fleas are absolutely tiny, they are one of the **strongest** animals in the world in relation to size, and can jump huge distances.

Flea jump

STRENGTHENS YOUR CORE MUSCLES AND LEGS.

Jump straight up as high as you can, then land back in the squat position.

Start in a relaxed squat position.

WADDLE

like a penguin

These birds live in icy areas. Their feet
are webbed, which is great for swimming,
but isn't great for walking, so when they
are on land penguins **waddle slowly**
so they don't slip on the ice.

Did you know?

After a female emperor
penguin lays an egg, she
goes of for food and the
male balances the egg
on his feet to keep it
warm and safe.

Don't slip!

Penguin shuffle

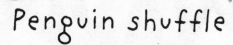

STRENGTHENS YOUR CORE
MUSCLES AND SHOULDERS.

Start by standing with your feet
together and your arms slightly
pointing out to the side.

Point your toes outwards and
take short, shuffling steps while
keeping your heels together.

Challenge yourself
Try balancing a ball on
your feet as you walk,
as if it is an egg!

Swing your arms up and
down for balance as you go.

SETTLING DOWN MEDITATIONS

Here are some two minute meditations to perform before bed that will help get you mentally ready for sleep.

Use your imagination to put yourself in the place of an animal in each environment. While doing so, focus on your breathing, inhaling in slowly through the nose, and out through the mouth.

SIGHT

SOUND

TOUCH

MONDAY: Desert

If you were a camel in a **scorching hot desert**, what would your senses experience? Close your eyes, breathe, and transport your mind…

 A light wind causing the grains of sand to blow around in all directions.

 Sand dunes, bright sunlight, clear blue skies.

 Intense heat, warm air, loose sand under your feet.

TUESDAY: Ocean

If you were a whale in the **vast ocean**, what would your senses experience? Close your eyes, breathe, and transport your mind…

 Crashing waves, whales singing to each other.

 The blue of the water, rolling waves, ships, fish, and other ocean creatures.

 Currents of cold water all around.

WEDNESDAY: Jungle

If you were a python in **a tropical jungle**, what would your senses experience? Close your eyes, breathe, and transport your mind…

Branches and twigs snapping, leaves rustling, insects buzzing, birds chirping.

The green canopy, leaves, earthy ground, trees, animals everywhere.

Sssss…

Thick humidity, the warmth of the air, dirt from the earth.

THURSDAY: Mountains

If you were an eagle **soaring over mountain peaks**, what would your senses experience? Close your eyes, breathe, and transport your mind…

 Strong wind, whistling air, birds calling out.

The white of the snowy mountain tops, clear blue sky, mist around the mountains, trees below.

 Cold air being blown by the wind.

FRIDAY: The Arctic

If you were a polar bear in the **freezing Arctic**, what would your senses experience? Close your eyes, breathe, and transport your mind...

Whistling wind, snow crunching underneath your feet.

The white of the snow and ice, blue sea, your breath turning to steam.

Freezing wind blowing against you, soft snow beneath your feet.

SATURDAY: Waterfall

If you were a wild horse beneath **a cascading waterfall**, what would your senses experience? Close your eyes, breathe, and transport your mind...

The deafening rush of water, bubbles of air popping and rising to the surface.

Falling water, bubbles, wet rocks behind the water, spray in the air.

The damp from the water spray, wet feet from the rocks.

SUNDAY: Beach

If you were a starfish on a **peaceful beach**, what would your senses experience? Close your eyes, breathe, and transport your mind…

 A light breeze, waves crashing, bubbles popping on the sand.

 Golden sand, blue sea, reflected sky, colourful fish, crabs, and shells.

 The heat of the sun, coolness of the wet sand.

DK LONDON

Author Radzi Chinyanganya
Illustrator Francesca Rosa
Acquisitions Editors James Mitchem, Sam Priddy
Senior Designer Rachael Parfitt Hunt
Senior Production Editor Robert Dunn
Senior Production Controller Ena Matagic
Jacket Co-ordinator Issy Walsh
Senior Jacket Designers Jo Clark, Rachael Parfitt Hunt
Jacket Photographer Lol Johnson
Creative Director Helen Senior
Publishing Director Sarah Larter

DK DELHI

Asst Art Editor Simran Lakhiani
Project Editor Kanika Kalra
Managing Art Editor Ivy Sengupta
DTP Designers Ashok Kumar, Satish Gaur,
Vikram Singh, Sachin Gupta
Asst Picture Research Administrator Vagisha Pushp

First published in Great Britain in 2021 by
Dorling Kindersley Limited
DK, One Embassy Gardens,
8 Viaduct Gardens,
London, SW11 7BW

A CIP catalogue record for this book is
available from the British Library.
ISBN: 978-0-2414-5308-7

Printed and bound in the UK

For the curious
www.dk.com

A message from Radzi:

THANK YOU!!! I am incredibly proud
of this book, but it's not mine, it's ours:

Francesca Rosa, the INCREDIBLE illustrator
who brought my ideas to life. DK, the dream team
publishers who fully believed in the concept. Alex,
Henry, and Hannah, who have tirelessly taken
it from root to fruit. Youth Sport Trust for the
fantastic work they do, and for inspiring the germ
of the idea. My Mum and Sister Rufaro, for always
being them. But most importantly, thank YOU for
allowing me to share with you my love of movement.

About the author:

Radzi Chinyanganya has been presenting television
for over 10 years, including flagship shows such as
Blue Peter, Crufts, the Paralympics, and Winter
Olympics. Prior to this he was a top 10 GB skeleton
bobsleigh athlete and has always had a passion for
inclusivity around fitness and exercise. In 2017,
Radzi was announced as an ambassador for Super
Movers, a campaign to encourage kids to move as
they learn. With a stint on Dancing on Ice in 2020,
Radzi can also be regularly seen presenting
athletics, snooker, tennis, strongman events and
wrestling, to name a few, as well as movie premieres
for much loved children's classics such as The Lion
King and Toy Story 4. You can follow him on Twitter,
Instagram, and TikTok as @iamradzi.

DK would like to thank:

Sam Priddy and Jo Clark for kicking off this
fantastic book. Alex Fisher and Henry Thorpe of
M&C Saatchi Merlin and Hannah Weatherill of
Northbank Talent. Tori Ball for make up. Emma
Lane for styling. Hayley Cox and Jamie Elby for
PR and marketing. Most of all, thanks to Radzi
for his vision, creativity, and endless enthusiasm.

The publisher would like to thank the following for their
kind permission to reproduce their photographs:

(Key: a-above; b-below/bottom; c-centre; f-far; l-left;
r-right; t-top)

123RF.com: smileus 58bl, Yuliia Sonsedska 56bl; **Dorling
Kindersley:** Blackpool Zoo, Lancashire, UK 68tc, 68bl,
69cra, Jerry Young 28tr, 28br, 30tr, 30br, 31bl, 61tc, 79 (x3),
80–81 (x7), 90 (x7); **Dreamstime.com:** Kseniya Abramova
/ Tristana 94cb, Amwu 46b, Ziga Camernik 18bl, Iakov
Filimonov / Jackf 76c, Eric Isselee 52tr, 52b, 64b, Isselee
50tr, Jgade 60tr, Liliia Khuzhakhmetova 89b, Tom
Linster / Flinster007 93c, Xavier Marchant /
Xaviermarchant 90cra, Menno67 92c. Grondin Franck
Olivier 71tl, Pixworld 42bl, S100apm 82, Seadam 62
(x3), Kucher Serhii 57bl, Vladvitek 16; **Fotolia:**
Willee Cole 38bl, Dixi 39tc, Eric Isselee 65tr,
66tl, 67tr; **Getty Images:** Mike Kemp 21tr,
21bl; **Getty Images / iStock:** Olha_stock 24bl,
proxyminder 20tr, 20c (x3)

All other images © Dorling Kindersley
For further information see: www.dkimages.com